THIS

Is Written

in the Stars

office@solaceandshine.ca

www.sivanihowe.ca

ISBN: 978-1-9990541-5-1

10 9 8 7 6 5 4 3

Published by Solace & Shine Publishing

SOLACE&SHINE
PUBLISHING

*This book is for Phrono
and all the souls whose
hearts yearn for the home
we cannot name.*

Contents

*remembering

*reckoning

*reconciling

*rebirth

acknowledgements

To the Lightbeings, seen and unseen, who guide and support, who push me (just a little) and who shine a light on the path towards more beauty in this human existence than I could ever dream.

I'd also like to thank my beloved husband Wally who has been on this wild ride with me throughout this chapter. It may have taken us to the end of sanity, but man has it brought us closer.

To my sweet son Narayana who writes the best Haiku and who makes me laugh every single day.

To Adam whose support and keen eye to the craft gave me the encouragement to bring it home.

To Saumya for your heartbeats, encouragement and eye for beauty and detail. I thank you.

I'd like to thank Rosie, Ash, Steve and the girls at Lairbeck where I wrote many of these poems.

To Omshanti for being the best poetry cheerleader and a master of the emoji sentence, and to all of my community who read drafts and shared with me how you experienced these capsules.

And lastly, but not least, to him, for standing with me in the pouring rain -- I've never been happier.

Foreword by Adam Walker PhD

Sivani Howe's *THIS is Written in the Stars* is not just a collection of poems; it charts a journey of transformation. It is a deeply personal and sometimes enigmatic chronicle of a change of heart, a verbal record of alteration that guides the reader through the labyrinth of inner experience.

As records, the poems are acts of remembrance. Some serve as cenotaphs for past utterances, while others stand as shrines or signposts that stabilize into recognizing past experiences. Her poems are as much about remembering as they are about reconciling what is lost with what is found in growth. More than merely commemorative, the poems are written with an awareness of the performative power of poetry. They aspire not only to *represent* certain experiences of transformation, but to also *perform* those experiences.

The poems are to be experienced in whole, as a network of moments that coordinate a larger experience. The flow mirrors the transformation: things fall apart, we confront our loss, we heal, and then we rise anew, altered but whole. In this sense, the poetic character of *THIS* is that of the elegy; its enactments are organized according to the elegiac progression from loss to a discovery of what the speaker of John Milton's "Lycidas" called a "large recompense."

In English poetry, there is a precedent for the poetics that *THIS* develops in its own way. The notion that spiritual experience can be encoded into the shape of sound and meaning can readily be found in a strain of poetics that emerged out of the English Renaissance, especially in the devotional mode. This aspect of poetry has been comparatively overlooked by literary critics and academic poetry workshops alike. Perhaps it is something that cannot be easily described, much less taught. But it remains a unique virtue of the verbal art of lyric poetry. One of the most well known poets who revitalized an awareness of this virtue was the Victorian poet Gerard Manley Hopkins, who attempted to communicate what he called the "thisness" of things into verse. The revival of this virtue characterizes Romantic and post-Romantic verse, traditions of which many contemporary poets are inheritors.

All this is to say that Śivani's experiment is in good company while, at the same time, her poetry is underivative and uniquely her own. These poems channel both the intensity and tenderness of the human spirit. Through authentic imagery, emotional depth, and occasional playfulness and humor, *THIS* paints a portrait of spiritual change that is at once deeply personal and uniquely fresh.

- Adam Walker, PhD, October 2024

let me take you on a journey...

THIS is Written in the Stars, is a capsule of light that maps my journey of a mind-bending, life-trembling transformation, where both my lower and higher minds were woven through an experience of my heart breaking open and then blooming into its fullest expression –– embodying the Presence of Love.

THIS... is my ode to Love itself while showing how my journey manifested along the way as heartbreak tempered by duty, care bolstered by memories of lifetimes past, and hard decisions that required copious amounts of courage. These things combined lead me to a seat at the table of pure magic.

I offer *THIS...* to you here as a map to inspire your own journey, to console, to encourage and to balm your heart so that you do not feel alone in your own awakening from the mundane 3D into an embodied 5D reality.

THIS... is not a map giving direction, but a map of permission for you to experience your treasure hunt towards finding your own heart's unique expression.

THIS... holds a transmission of both remembrance and evolution. It encapsulates the memories of a period of time when everything was given, ripped away, and then made better, slowly, as though my life was a living kintsugi artwork.

This period of time in my life was an intense, beautiful, consuming, and devastating chapter where I consciously experienced each moment in what seemed like three different timelines or realities simultaneously. The first as a series of linked, past life memories. The second, a present life experience where both lower and higher minds were vying for the narrative between what has always been, and what could be. And the third, an overlaid Cosmic hand guiding the whole experience and wrapping each (sometimes excruciating) moment in the most exquisite experience of Love or, what I call, THIS.

THIS required me to question every belief I've held and to re-examine every aspect of my patriarchal, cultural conditioning. THIS asked me to "up my game" in ways I had never been required, or capable of, before. Each thread had the same souls, the same connections, playing out through different aspects of Self which supported my unfolding and eventual blossoming.

The result was a metamorphosis. A permanent change in who I am, and how I relate to –– reality. A change where I was, by Grace and by grit, able to emerge with an awakened heart.

I offer *THIS is Written in the Stars* here to honor the moment; to remember it; and to keep it real before time morphs the memories.

I have used *i* in these works to denote the perspective of the lower-mind, and *I* to denote the high-mind. *You* is used for the cosmic guidance while *He, he* and *you* represent the illusional "other."

All characters and voices in these poems are my reality/perspective giving form to my heart's journey of breaking open, of de-conditioning, of connection and attachment, of codependency, of kindness, of grief and, ultimately, of the Presence of Love.

remembering

Directions to THIS

So you want directions to THIS do you?
OK, I will tell you, but be warned, you
likely won't survive the journey –– i didn't.

Put down your pen and paper,
for you must commit each step to heart.
Focus your mind on what I say,
so you don't stray into the doldrums
of depression,

      desperation,

            and despair.

Now, listen carefully,
for I'll say this just once.
Set out at dawn
as soon as you hear
Robins sing the light into day.
Take a left at need,
keep walking past want, and

cross the road just before desire.

You definitely want to give that nook a
wide berth; lest you dwindle.

Soon enough, you'll come to a
pretty shiny door
on an unassuming house.
Face it head on,
and then without hesitation,
turn 180 and don't look back.

Breathe

Squint far into the distance.
There you'll see Willow's humble
boughs, bowing deeply — go there.
Once you are standing
at a little spring flowing
at Sally's gnarly feet,
bring your palms together
and slowly spin clockwise

       three whole rotations

while murmuring 13 'thank you's' to Her.

Then drip a little water on your crown,

and drink deeply, for the rest of the journey

lays in draught.

From Sally's Spring

stand on the wooden bridge;

look westward to Sun setting

beyond the hills that zig the W of worthy.

Make a beeline for the middle crest

and when you get to seemingly endless

Blackberry brambles on old Harry's

fence-line, there's a gate

            108 steps to the right.

Use that, but be sure to close it

behind you, and for God's sake,

resist the urge to partake

in midnight drupelets.

Just

  keep

    walking –– in silence now

Cease your incessant humming,

your unconscious mental mumbling.

You need to be fully present for this last part.

Keep your eye on the horizon with every step

and at the moment Sun kisses Land,

                      drop to your knees.

Smell the green grass of gratitude,

and sing Her song of praise,

until your heart cries out for the

wonder before you.

Offer your tears to the spot

where you find your-Self,

until your frame shakes itself awake,

snot runs and you feel

it is now OK to die.

Look around

Is your sight soft now?

Can you see the poetry in problems;

hear the silent beauty beyond

the boisterousness of Man?

Can you feel an invisible Presence

embracing you,

emanating from you?

Yes? Then you have arrived in THIS.

Here, now, breathe deeply and

decide.

✦

THIS is the hard part

It's 3am when i crawl back into bed.
I've domed him, his mother, his sister,
on the other side of the world,
in a golden orb to protect from
suicidal souls with stories to tell
at funerals.

You stand at the foot of my bed
cloaked, in my wedding quilt
i lay next to my beloved.
I feel him echoed in two lovers past.
i sacrificed myself for, both
i walked away from.

He will need you, You say
I will love him, I know
THIS might destroy me
neither of us dares admit.
In the dark I see clearly,

THIS is the promise

for digesting the poison.

You feel like home,

from a world i can't return to - yet

five words uttered,

fallacy maybe, but they

smell to me of freedom.

THIS is the hard part.

✦

higher perspective

She doesn't understand what's to come,
doesn't know her world's foundation
left five years back, doesn't realize
she's been treading water all this time.
She can feel it now though,

the fatigue from trying to float.

She daydreams about drowning,
well trained in non-attachment,
doesn't realize I can hear her.

But she'd never do that –– can't do that.
See, her boy holds her acutely
when her mind runs obtuse.

She knows she has things to do there
–– we do, pivotal to the mission
she has to get through this, and

THIS has to get through to her.

She's already amputated limbs
before -- twice -- with a spoon,
the last times the portal aligned,
the last times she could feel me close.

I watched her do it thinking
it was about the Toronto boy,
then the Australian boy, but

it's never been about them.

She was fierce in her 20's
more than most souls I've seen.
Now, she's less fierce -- more happy,
and I'm happy I've finally come back for her,

so she can hold him,

steady him, while his heart skips
she will need to let go

of all she thinks of as normal.

Yet, I know she can do it, after all,

I still have the spoon.

✦

space

Sometimes precious things fall apart
—— like hearts, disintegrate
like Magic Sand,

making space for things
we never imagined were missing,
people we didn't know we needed.

✦

merkabahs

i didn't think it was possible

to sit on my deck, at home

in the spring light of May,

and see a room half a world away.

He's having a rough day, his heart's

skipping, i'm worried, I dome him,

the only way I can help

too far away to show him.

Frn says, *call in a Merkabah,*

then shows me how it is done,

now I'm in a house I don't recognize

across the world my mind has come.

I see stairs to the right,

a living room to the side,

I walk up step by step, now

on the landing I turn and glide

to a room lit in turquoise

where a team of guides stand,

he's trying to rest now

together we do what we can.

If you can help, help

they say

if you can give, give

they offer

if you can serve, serve

they implore

if you can offer solace, do.

But don't sacrifice

yours in the process,

it's the only thing you can't

afford to lose.

- guess what i did

✦

re-member

To remember this place I've never been ––
it's strange, to remember him, somehow
I can exhale now, as THIS feels closer to home
on the other side of the world.

I'm emotional as I make breakfast, happily
listening for signs of life; I hold the portal open
so he can feel something beyond his fallible heart,
beyond the boundaries of his boxed beliefs.

I feel something too, need it, too,
to breathe, to slow down.
I hear music here.
Is there magic here?
Am I illusional?
Is THIS you?

            us?

                  me?

for the moment –– a mystery.

His walls are bare; the gardens are barren.

So slowly, we plant lavender to calm the heart,

slowly, we hang art; then he rests while I

furnish the patio following his burnable plans.

I help him make his house a home

while mine's being rigged with explosives.

It's his heart that's lost its rhythm,

but it's mine that is preparing to be told of Afib.

He's never laid on the grass,

never been held by the Mother.

never looked at Land like a lover;

and I talk to him like I always have,

for all the lifetimes before. Never been able to hide

from him I bare my honesty like I'm removing a habit.

I dress for dinner listening to the Light whispering

their wisdom that I'm on the right track;

that the end will always be dressed in regret.

But THIS moment demands we both play our parts

to perfection, so he can feel held while he falls apart;

so I can finally re-member mySelf.

mill ponds and magic

Horses run wild in New Forest,
where Trees have been forever.

His heart races and skips, flushing his face,
as he walks, slightly wobbly, to a spot in the sun

where we both hope to call in the Light.
We sit and picnic and talk about the

whys of the world; and the hows of the heart.
It's hard to let go of familiar shadows,

ones that have always kept us safe, and hidden.
But Past's cousin Fear, loves to death grip beliefs,

then spiral them into stories that no longer hold true,
churning them into dis-ease. Turning inward,

we close our eyes to perceive clearly a reality beyond
the senses, and entrain our breath to slow the rhythm of time.

The Portal opens and Frn's mill-pond of stillness floods us both

in otherworldly Peace, as Sun's light cloaks us in Remembrance.

Later he relays that he thought he felt my heart stop.

Smiling, I tell him, *when the Portal opens, sometimes I go*

to a place where hearts don't need to beat to be alive.

Finally relaxed, he feels fine for the first time in weeks;

realizes entrainment and mill-ponds are magic manifest.

I realize all energy in this realm must go somewhere as

my heart starts to race and skip, flushing my face.

I walk, slightly wobbly, back from where we came,

telling myself, the key thing is

-- he's feeling better.

✦

there's bees in the buttercup veld

There's bees in the buttercup veld

whispering to the heart, breathe

Love, beat and be present,

at home without a house,

connected without converse.

Dragonflies delicately weave starseed

blue between wildflowers

surrendering to light; dancing

in sunlit grass to melodies

humans long to hear.

The buttercup veld needs no words as

hearts skip –– race; then stop altogether.

Suspending time in unstruck sound.

For there's nothing to push against here,

not in the buttercup veld.

✦

entrainment

I put my hand on his erring heart
and hold his hand on mine.
Frn balms us both in the mill-pond,
then You flood me with
distant earthquakes he can feel.

Stargates open and THIS
permeates the air the way
incense sanctifies a temple.

It feels like home he says softly;
my being sings with remembrance,
his turns to stone like
there's snakes in my hair.

+

blueprint

Sitting here with tea in hand,
who am i kidding, it's coffee,
I'm looking out to the Rockie's expanse
under Summer's dawn sky remembering
the time I watched a new blueprint be branded
on a heart in the colour blanketed above me.

As i flew to him, a dearest friend,
Anam Cara, in some circles –– unable to survive a box,
we stood together in the ether, Phrono and Bradley
and I, bearing witness to his heart's birthday as a
layer of light, an intricate weaving of luminous lace,
was cast into the mantle of his being.

It was a wondrous moment to watch a birthday womb-side;
and like all good and worthy life quests, it will take time
to bloom, for him to be able to smell the sweet fragrance of the
Presence of Love emanating from within.
But if it's nurtured, like a hedge maze, it will grow and
guide him to the centre of Self.

I'll be there in a few hours, I said to him that day before my Spirit

left his side, *I'm looking forward to seeing you.*

He smiled and followed me back to the Merkabah,

to the cliffs where the Light disperses. Amused, I returned

him to his body, laying in the hospital,

while mine was hurtling over the Atlantic in a tin can,

returning to Albion shores, for THIS.

✦

downstairs, upstairs

Downstairs

he stands at the front door

heart in rhythmic song,

he smiles, hugs me

his mother looks on.

Upstairs

luggage rests

he turns to me

we embrace,

and in Your arms

I am home.

✦

wild flowers

In the depths of the herb garden

bordered by a wild-flower veld,

as we lay in essence, bare

beneath Moon's full heart,

both flooded in Re:membrance. That's when

I told You I would come back with him.

I can't comprehend even now, how

the waters of THIS carve canyons

only for us. A hallowed place where

words echo in a language not spoken;

wrap sounds in colours beyond song. It's where

You told me I will need to come back to him.

Imprinted on marrow

yet forgotten by mind

a force unseen pulls us together

–– and rips me apart,

for Happiness Does Not Wait, it quietly

lingers in the shadows of longing. It's why I came back

for him –– for You,

and I have.

✦

the presence

To sit in the Presence of Love,

that's what was required.

To remember a connection,

measured in lifetimes –– not months,

to reconnect to the depth of my Being

–– in transcendence.

That's what held his heart steady,

while he sang silently for her;

while I stood by my beloved.

THIS presence required me to

recognize a Love unheard of,

demanded i face it,

embrace it, embody it,

keep showing up for it and

now –– reconcile it.

It's Love's expression,

not reflection that heals.

Sunlight brings growth,

Moonlight balms,

Lovelight spans time,

spans space,

spans worlds.

Oh beautiful, sweet, unconditional Love!

You heal hearts, hold them steady,

break them - open, and yet, still,

you cannot connect two that are

dreaming in different dimensions.

✦

reckoning

bloody Sunday

A gift offered gets marked,

scaring the paper in blue

lines, drawn in sand with

mines buried each side. Now

neither of us can move

and survive as we were.

I don't know what I want,

but i know it's not THIS,

his honesty somersaults,

but Anam Cara this is precious,

valuable -- to me.

i leave my body to halfway

somewhere before the

cap is even on the marker.

No longer welcome here,

perhaps i never was,

only what I bring:

a sherpa of light, a lifeline of solace.
But it is THIS I have come for
perhaps not him after all.
I wonder if he sees the
trainwreck dead ahead.

✦

who are you?

Who are you
if not the woman who
dances in puddles
barefoot in the rain?

Who are you
if not the woman who
giggles in sunshine and
takes away my pain?

- he asks

✦

walk away

I will need to walk away

You say,

But not yet, first...

I must return,

hold my heart open

        no matter what comes,

stand in my higher mind

        no matter what goes,

and when the time is right

Remember,

You say,

I will need to be the one to walk away.

✦

the suspended log

It's early fall, and Night's air,

crisp but not yet chilled,

kisses our cheeks as

we sit on a suspended log,

like us, a balancing act

where the fun is in falling off.

i almost died, i say into the darkness,

i know, he says sweetly,

Does he even care?

the breeze whispers between us.

A prayer to be held

murmurs from my marrow;

i have to ask for a hug.

✦

terminal

Loving him,

like facing a terminal illness,

I find joy for joy's sake.

Take pictures with my mind

every moment, soften

to memories made in real time.

Knowing there is no future,

I find beauty in

Loving –– him.

✦

like it was yesterday

I remember healing with herbs the fevers

few deemed survivable;

my songs sweetening the passage of birth.

I remember being hauled down

dark halls to dungeons;

flogged in a stone cell sour with death.

✦

conflict

— as read by David Attenborough

It's 2024.

The middle-aged white man
stands in the sun at the window,
hands in pockets,
looking out to a world
he doesn't recognize as his.

i don't like conflict, he declares
as a gentlemanly virtue.

*Maybe 'cause you've never had to
fight for anything, it always gets handed to you,*

says the eternal woman standing behind him,
looking over his patriarchal shoulder,
settling for secondhand sunlight.

✦

only the winds

We talk in low light

'cause, neither of us want to see

what has become.

                Back and forth

the conversation circles over our arc

when that song comes on

                      you know the one.

Neither of us break stride when it starts

like it doesn't matter

                but it matters

'cause you don't talk over the voice of the Holy,

you don't natter while an Angel cries. So slowly,

without signal, our stream of words -- suspend

The first cry opens the portal to

the second, pries

the third, threatens - us

and the fourth breaks - me.

The fifth mourns, while the sixth sets you free,

and by the time the seventh finally remembers

                    -- we no longer exist.

The eighth and ninth cry softly over our suspended words;

float them hopelessly, on the single remaining string

while we sit, in the dark, watching them swoon

in the single shard of lamplight, dust

slow dancing in the echoes of THIS

until finally, silence weeps.

✦

amputation preparation

He never saw me, for me
i don't know what he saw, i guess
we both saw what we needed,
until we both saw what we didn't.

✦

yellow roses

yellow roses
bodyguard and pal
like the old song
Betty and Al

but

he didn't protect me;
we're no longer friends
and all the yellow roses
died in the end.

✦

dare to dream

he may think I'm mad,

but I know I'm madly alive

on levels he won't dare to dream.

the ? at the eleventh hour

The tea is too hot

... but where is THIS all going?

geese fly westward, home

✦

at the top of the stairs

At the top of the stairs
we can't get any higher,
standing between rooms,
between worlds, we embrace

one more time.

Like clockwork
the Stargate opens, and
my world dissolves
into the void of
THIS
Cosmic
Love.
Letting go, deaths replay
themselves over and over,
lifetimes and lifetimes --
once upon again

only "the end" remains,

'till he pulls away

shocked, in a flash

of Blue, I'm left standing

alone on the landing

with You.

✦

past lives collide

i short circuit at the thought of him,

relive the meteor strike

so beautiful

so deadly, i died

over and over

in his arms,

on the dark wet curb,

buzzing on gin

remembering other lifetimes

when loving him

was a sin.

THAT was the hard part

I rise surrounded by

Red Rocks and Cottonwoods with

yesterday's eclipse still reverberating

through marrow and mind.

Now, You say, *It's time to walk away.*

Handing me a spoon You disappear.

No reception's no excuse,

so alone I drive to the highway

to bars with no holds.

People here are driving towards,

driving away - with limbs intact, oblivious

Ms Roadrunner scuttles around the truck

hunting snacks, unaware of the soul surgery

about to take place before her.

Number dialed. Our connection's unstable

like a dead man walking, so we chat.

Explaining's the incision,

understanding's the pain, and

when words have been

exhausted and the bone's been cut

through, it ends in his polite punctuation:

We can still be friends.

(like that's not what we were all along)

As the last string of sinew's severed – –

in silence,

the call reluctantly disconnects.

My world starts to spin

and just as I begin to bleed out,

You arrive out of nowhere –

a tourniquet of light.

He needed you, You say

I love him, I whisper, *and*

THIS has destroyed me.

Both of us can see there's a

certain beauty at the heart

of destruction.

Five words uttered,
flushing me with an air
of congratulations, like
I've made it to some illusive
threshold of freedom.

THAT was the hard part.

✦

my unworthiness

died while hiking to the Seven Sacred Pools in Sedona AZ on the 15th October 2023 at the age of 44. Bathed in the auspicious frequency of a 5 - freedom was finally achieved after a long battle with impostor syndrome. As fate politely closed the door on the house entrusted to 1987, destiny lit a match and burned it to the ground. i can't tell you what it looked like as it caved in on itself. I didn't have the heart to turn around -- if I had, i might have run back in. But I can tell you that it smelt of cornflower tea with lavender and it sounded like the roar of an away crowd scoring the winning goal.

+

have you got THIS?

Have You got this?
Have You got THIS?
Have i just survived an amputation
only to slowly drown in grief?

Each footfall i hike pounds
my question into the orange dust
as I look to Starseeds for answers;
as i cry silently beneath Noonday Sun.

Have you got me?
Will I find THIS?
Again, *have i just cut off my*
only connection to my Cosmic home?

Have I got this? You say,
your sudden presence,
an extended hand
to my drowning heart.

Have I got THIS?

I am THIS... You are THIS,

> *We were THIS all along.*

I stop walking to make my ears hear clearer.

Focus on the ground in front of me as though

I have just seen it flicker in liquid ripples.

Every cosmic calibration was your own heart reflected,

You say, *every stargate was our connection colliding,*

every Divine moment seared into your memory

will be your heart's song manifest.

> *So sit now... and Sing.*

reconciling

hadar cazimi

Go for a walk –– they say,
the land will cheer you up, gently
hold your grief –– help heal your heart.
So i put my Poncho on, boots and gloves, slowly
i walk to the spillway to scream
and sob into Stream ice-cold.

Stalks of Wild-Rose maroon catch my eye,
snacked down to thorny stubs next to Evergreen
Firs, who tower and declare that nothing has changed,
 –– but everything has changed. Walking the path
the air is crisp, scrubbing my mind and memory
still, i think of You

Boulders mapped in lichen and
marked in islands of pale green moss,
speak of adventures decades in the making,
laying out a path of treasures, now
no one recognizes,
still, i search for You

Honey coloured grasses reach for

the unseen, I touch them with my frozen

fingers, so beautiful even though dead.

No one notices them until

they burn too easily,

still, i feel for You

Terracotta needles of Ponderosa Pine

halo the ground where vanilla permeates the air,

one step, two step, then gone. The scent pulls at me,

imploring me to walk in the past

hoping it can trick me into calling it the present,

still, i remember You

I meander in the grove of golden Larch where,

frosted white crystals on wild

Strawberry leaves crunch under foot.

Charred logs lay next to little red berries

not yet found by Bears,

still, i look for You

Crow caws, spotting me from above,

naming me friend or foe, i don't know,

i don't speak Crow. Pausing for a moment

–– i look up

and that's where I finally find You

in a flash of sky Blue.

- keep your chin up

✦

hold silence

Hold silence
l o n g
      e n o u g h
that you realize
the power, of
every
single
word.

✦

Replaced
forgotten,
discarded at warp speed.

Didn't qualify for a first thought,
–– let alone a second.

He's great
lighter now,
in Love
able to fly now,
to her
he shares with a twinkle of pride ––

i've let go of a lot of emotional baggage since we spoke last.

... and that's it, that's the moment i realize,
i've never been called

emotional baggage
to my face before.

✦

shrapnel

we sit together

an ocean away,

he's thinking it's going well,

i'm discretely picking out shrapnel,

so not to dampen the mood

same moment

yet worlds apart

I'm forever lifting him up while

his callus shots never miss,

my blood seeps quietly onto the page.

all too soon

All too soon
he discarded THIS to the recycling
ripped up our masterpiece without question
gifting me my answer –– he never did care.

While i dissect each memory,
have each morsel nourish me;
evolve me, 'till I embody THIS gift,
the answer to my deepest prayer.

✦

no other

Hold your heart open,
don't close it to the hurt,
feel joy in his happiness,
don't take his quickness personally,

it's not about you, for him
it never was.
Extricate THIS
but don't discard him

the way you feel discarded,
for there is no other.
You live in a different world now
remember, one he cannot visit.

✦

whispers

When whispers are ignored,
and words are not believed,
when to inform is to be doubted
and to call out is to be deemed –– a liar.

When cries of frustration are rendered as fragile,
and screams of indignation are labeled: bitch,
when one declaration for action is over dramatic;
healing with herbs gets branded a witch.

To want to be left alone
is declared eccentric and unstable,
to live as One with forest friends as family
gets condemned to the pyre, not given a gable.

Knew they was no good, cry the masses,
knew they was mad –– crazy –– lunatic,
if they had only said something sooner
we would have beat them with a stick.

Now sweet faggots of friends are stacked, betraying

towns people gather in the square by the well,

Love burns alive staring them all down in silence,

knowing loose tongues and deaf fears are already living in hell.

i miss...

i sit housebound,

paralyzed on a shingled island

in a sea of ice and mud,

dreaming of a place once known.

You say,

to miss something

is to love it from afar,

so I'll tell you what I miss.

I miss watching Sun rising

over the padlocked wooden gate as

Geese fly overhead –– westward

like clockwork –– it must be 07:30

Standing, cradling a coffee,

bathing in the light of Ascent –– Day One

the memory, it brings me back to life,

one ivory at a time.

it was real

THIS single piece of music

invokes the sublimation of my heart,

rendering its Ascent-ion into states

overwhelming: expanding the Self

beyond Clouds to meander

amongst Stars, while

simultaneously

plummeting my being

into crippling pain.

Such extremes stretch me, until,

even now, months later, everything disappears

and only the Presence of Love remains,

-- that's how I know

it was real.

train wreck

We were three months out from our destination
when we passed the hamlet of Bloody Sunday.
Stumbling wearily to the rear carriage of the train,
I held each seat for stability as it
jolted and jostled over rail-joints.

Out the window I watched as the
writing on the wall morphed from a
mural of Robins and remembrance,
into a warning sign –– red, rigid and
wrapped in barbed wire. Carefully,

I wrapped my precious memories
in bubble wrap, stacked them
as far from the engine as possible,
padded them with disappointments,
buffered them with expectations not met;
covered them in a blanket of politeness.

No one wanted to make a scene.

As the train built momentum,

the heartbeat of rail-joints raced

to a climax of catastrophe, and

in what looked like months,

but felt like minutes,

my mind got etched with

the sound of burnt breaks,

the sight of metal screaming; and

the smell of windows shattering

got carved into my soul.

The crash was violent. But it was the silence

that followed that's been devastating.

I remember whispering sorry to the litter of memories

I couldn't protect as I was flung into the future

unable to grasp the moment. Coming to,

exposed and alone, there's been nothing to do but

slowly recover, see what's held true,

guess at what was discarded in the impact;

try and remember what I can't find.

I'm sorry

I kept repeating, as though I had just one simple job,
remember-protect-entrain-inspire--save.
I picked up all the pieces I could walk away with;
glued them together with gold-dust and tears
and pretend I'm happy with the results.

I hold now in my hand shards of moments:
A smell, a smile, a perfectly cut strawberry;
I find a chunk of conversation hidden
under a park bench of my mind and
tell myself they are still beautiful -- broken.

I will always miss the wind and rain in my hair as
you watch me dance amongst the Standing Stones, our
meanders in meadows; decadent conversations that
devour time the way a candle consumes darkness.
But now, I sleep soundly to the lullaby of my own
gently beating heart and wake up to
Sunlight and Bluebirds at my window.

✦

beautiful

It broke a part of me
i thought i needed.
i'm still sitting,
looking at the
shattered pieces
basking in golden light.

Blood seeps from the Shiv,
silken rivulets
seeking new sanctuary,
pulsing to a drum i cannot hear.
If i close my eyes
the world slips into a

deep sense of expansion;
I look up to constellations,
shooting stars that died long ago.
Yet, even after they're gone
still their light I see;

I've never felt so beautiful.

excruciating

I look left, excruciating
sight right, bliss and bright
centered otherworldly
a glimpse of who I could be,

should be, will be, now
more me than ever before,
a stranger in the mirror,
I lie here on the floor.

Time's standing still
yet leaping in a blink,
peace comes in waves
when we see, not think.

I scream on the inside
smile on the surface, you say
the world is dying, I say *She's birthing,*
your laugh is nervous.

you always thought I was so tough

now I wiggle, waggle, womble

to music and red wine,

dancing to Gaia's rumble.

+

the playlist

Rhythmic additions to
the Ambient's become
my one-and-only sign his
heart's still beating. But,

beating doesn't mean
blossoming,
just like adding to
the Ambient
doesn't mean alive,

it just means not dead.

Which saddens me,
'cause for a time
the rhythm of his
beating heart was a
beautiful ambient
addition to my life;

one that opened mine.

of course

Of course
i shared with Moon and showed
Stars, the scars i have
from your words that cut

Of course
i wrangled Rain to hold my coffee
so i could whale upon Land about
what you did when i wasn't watching

Of course
i hit Her bark recklessly --
the way your silence hit my soul when i said
-- I love you

Of course
i pushed Wind out the way
so i could scream out to Sea about
how it felt to be cast aside

Of course

I'll write who you are to me,

into the Akash, immortalizing

the echoes of your taking.

- What did you want me to do?

✦

all in my head

Does it hurt not to dial my number

as much as it hurts not

to receive the call?

Perhaps it was all in my head,

but that's what you loved

wasn't it? My mind.

My words, not yours.

Yours were precious, but

whatever THIS was, it wasn't precious

enough for either of us to sustain -- the tight rope

between last time and THIS time,

never finding space and time for now.

So, I walked away, I grieved,

I mourned, and found myself

right back here, where I remembered --

Albion

Depression remembers

I try and tell my mind it's not rational;
that the grey clouds pushing down
on the land, a laden squall of grief
willing everything drowned, will pass.

But she's not listening.
She's too busy looking at her ashen dress,
sullen with floor dust and dried blood.
Once summer sky blue, it now expands
over the bare minimum of her morality,
exposing a dehiscent gash on her leg,
and an angry cut above her collarbone,
which her fingertips detect is infected.

She picks maggots off her thigh,
tries to conjure lavenders scent;
lays on the floor deflated.
She can't think her way out of the suffocating mix of hearsay
and betrayal coming from the rusted bucket in the corner,

so stolidly she watches the sliver of light coming through the bars, beyond her reach, yet hoof height above.

Light moves slowly across the stone,

a reverse hand on a clock,

turning back time,

highlighting smudges of blood and smatterings of slop,

punctuating the violent stench the room gestates.

Gauges trap shadows in the wall,

a carved letter here, a scratched symbol there,

pleas from the forsaken

not to be forgotten.

✦

your wise words

I miss how I felt around him;
I don't miss how he made me feel.

*That's because how you felt
had nothing to do with him.*

+

if i don't speak to you

If I don't speak to you

there is still room for you to be kind –– not callous,

for you to be happy, without the need to be cruel.

If I don't see you

there is still time for your eyes to soften –– to care,

for you to take your hands out of your damn pockets.

If I don't ask after you

there can still live my delicate memories,

–– precious and transcendent, not yet trampled by reality.

nameless

He was nameless, a love
transcending form and face,
I was nameless, a presence
not admitted to.

Spun my light as his own, then
wrote me out of his story,
so I'll write him into mine,
I'll say 'thank you',

I just won't say what for.

oh so polite

For ever and aye, after ample water
Under the bridge has flowed, your
Caring, sterile as land in drought, will
Keep historians baffled. Where

Yellow roses decayed to
Ochre and were offered to the ground, the
Undertakers will exhume what was said
Roll back the pages of text,

Pour over the syntax, and paint a picture
Of a fearful moth trapped in yesterday's jar.
Languishing from the search they will concede
Impartially, that your care was all English
Trite: politeness and palaver. Yet,
Even now, I am drawn to the Presence of Love in memory.
Navigated by duty, yet still saddened by colonialism
Electing to covet stolen gold, my tears will
Sprout beauty out of THIS, knowing my care
Sung in the Holy.

convenient

Capacity, or lack thereof, gives way to

Obliviousness relinquishing oneself from responsibility. It's

Not give and take with you - only take.

Verily, self-absorption is an

Excuse for overt disregard, so there's no

Need to show care beyond what's convenient. The

Inherent value of our

Enmeshed circumstance is a masterclass in

Navigating nuanced narcissism, so

Today I cry for us both.

✦

a coward dies many times

I've known a lot of cowards,

people plagued with the disease;

they demand respect and courtesy,

then dish volatility whenever they please.

I've watched their fear of pain

be the root of all suffering,

then require their children,

to inherently do the buffering.

Cowards always cry victim,

never taking responsibility;

they look at others, never the mirror,

too ashamed to sit in vulnerability.

I wonder if the coward dies many times,

or actually never lives,

never feels the sunlight of Truth on their face,

the warmth that honesty gives.

Cowards don't have the heart for empathy,

too paralyzed by narcissism,

to them hindsight stinks of guilt;

regret, their past built in Brutalism.

They spin a tale of a protector,

but a protector of whom, they'll never admit,

always trying to save face, one not worth saving,

you just end up waiting for the obit.

an honest apology

I'm sorry
I didn't hear you, didn't believe you
I thought you were being coy
–– attempting humility.

But I can see now,
see you were trying,
trying all along to tell me
–– that the beauty,

the magic I was experiencing
when we were together
had absolutely
nothing to do with you.

✦

surely

I want to say *thank you* and

I'll throw in an *I'm sorry* as well

for not acknowledging the

soul level

deep

cosmic love

from which you have come forth before me.

For surely,

it can only be out this place,

that someone would be willing

to play the role of *(insert noun here)*

so perfectly,

so faithfully, that it could incite a

healing, so deep, that it would

spark freedom.

✦

sometimes

Sometimes growing in the same direction
doesn't herald the results you hope.

Sometimes the friction of closeness
creates scars no one intended.

✦

bounce

I don't bounce like I used too
like I needed to
like you needed me to
like I thought I always should.

See, now I have no skin
I live everything –– 140%
sensitive to the senses;
porous to time.

I hear Trees sing;
I see the sonnets Wind whispers,
I feel the rope burn around my neck,
seared into the subconscious.

same story, different time

- the foreign light

He finds her on the dungeon floor,

locked in a reality of lack.

A bird cramped in a cage of conditioning,

he regards her with curiosity; she stares back.

He grips in one hand a scribbled note

citing the gift she holds, a map

to the answers of his fallible heart.

She lives in a different reality, he's told

If you help me, I'll share the map you seek,

They both look to the key he grasps,

crumpled on the floor she looks so meek.

He unlocks the iron's clasp.

Sunlight blinds her as she emerges

in her ruined dress disheveled from the dark,

just happy to be outside with the living,

the bird's alarm she does not hark.

The sweet breeze is marked, with the

stench of the wound she has festering.

Together they picnic on Lola's park bench,

then walk in a foreign light - unquestioning.

She lovingly gives him his answers

while they rest in the shade of wise Elder,

People stare at them, trying not to look,

like they have something important to tell her.

She breathes freely, finally, trusting,

inhaling wildflowers in the veld –– Divine.

Her heart swells with happiness as she lays there

replaying her luck. He notes her presence slows time.

Linking arms they meander through the hamlet

along quaint roads of cobblestone,

towards the sound of a thirst-quenching fountain,

the people passing now whisper in low tones.

Rounding the corner into Sunday Square

they're faced with a pyre and a crowd of people.

A sculpture, he tells her, not a structure,

as his friends close in from the shadow of the steeple.

He looks confused, laments like a lamb
that he clearly doesn't know what is real,
sheepishly offers a swig of his gin;
thanks her for her gift, says he loves her zeal.

Hoping his gratitude's a waiver for what's coming,
he implores her not to fuss,
'case her blaze puts him in a harsh light,
reminds her he's done only what he must.

He turns and leaves, never looking back,
while her body burns he seeks his next answers.
She imagines him following her map
to the Tor where his heart finally stirs.

She closes her eyes, conjures wise Elder,
leaves behind the dungeon's incarceration.
Rises a foreign light to be basked in - unquestioning,
as he walks tomorrows happily towards liberation.

✦

still

I'm too soft for this world.
Still, I pry my heart open
every morning, make myself care.

Look at this year from every angle,
dissect the morsels worth digesting
try not to retch at the rest.

I take responsibility –– someone has to,
berate myself for being gullible, for thinking
consideration and care wasn't too much to ask.

Still, I yearn for what was
my light reflected,
and call it your potential.

Still, I hope for gentle words
as I unlatch your sabred tongue.
Still, I crave your hug

even as you recoil from my touch.

I watch you, even now, use my good

nature to your advantage, and still

I wish you well.

+

perhaps

Perhaps my poems offend you

because I paint them with your words,

gild their frames with the stuff of your behavior.

Perhaps my poems upset you

because it's the first time someone has held

a mirror for you; not just a flame.

✦

sitting rigid

I'm here   sitting rigid

a sardine in a tin can

hurtling through the night

back to Heath's Row,

while down there, in a home

                                untouchable

in the depths of my mind, and

buried in a part of my heart

I can't seem to extract,

we sit in darkness

drinking tea

close, but not touching

                                sitting rigid

against the side of the Ottoman.

Do you know

how many countries

came together

to push them out?

Did they feel how I do here?

       exiled

Did they too have good intentions?

       rejected

For everyone's the hero in their story

        'til they're not.

Let me say... no,

let me ask...

do you miss it?

       sitting rigid,

hoping I don't push too far,

me, praying I don't get pushed,

both of us seeking solace on eggshells.

Drinking tea   in the dark

was to breathe freely after intubation.

I showed you my hand,

believed you would hold it gently,

but you chose   to sit rigid,

let them do what they wanted, to me

all our preciousness was

    slaughtered by the empire.

nothing more to say

Tomorrow I'm exhaling
holding no plans to return
to where the blinds are drawn,
to where I got burned.

My sympathetic's ramping up
gearing to scream her alarm,
inhale or die! admittedly
has a certain charm.

But Breath's promise is what
spurs on life;
her execution's what
quells the heart,

so I'll submerge the body
but not the face,
smile a smile
that leaves no trace

of my wish for time to stop

for the tea to steep

with confessions in the dark

before we sleep.

To be faced with midnight blue

bathed in a flickering glow

is Yellow Rose rooted? I wonder.

there's only one thing I know

tonight, sleep won't come

and tomorrow won't stay away

and for now

there's nothing more to say.

✦

rebirth

in 2 minds

If nothing is forgotten,
everything
then, must be forgiven.

If everything is remembered
nothing
then, is there to forgive.

✦

resolution

– as read by David Attenborough

It's 2024.

A middle-aged white woman
soaks in her cast-iron cauldron
heated by fire,
as Spring's sweet breeze
dances over her knees and shoulders,
soaking her in the remedy required.

I'm done with conforming, conditioning,
with patriarchy's pilfering.
She murmurs, her incantation setting the ground ready
to rumble in resolve.

Satisfied, she rests her head back and
crosses her ankles over the side of the tub;
basks the golden glow of Sunlight as it gently
caresses her skin directly.

broken/changed

Each moment, witnessing my humanness as a
pin-ball, flying off, flying to -- reflexes reaching
for the Wizard's intuition, the eye in the storm.

Dizzy, I fall to my knees to beg for mercy,
but on the way down, between lips and mind,
my message morphs to murmurs of thank-you.

I cry for the dead, to feel
strangely alive, in the leela
the narrative's a fable.

I peer into the darkness
to see clearly, Galaxies guiding us,
Illuminated Beings –– Starseeds aglow.

Deeply contented, I rip off my skin and
howl a note at Sun, so Holy,
it births a new world.

I say I'm short circuiting, I'm broken, but

You crouch in kindness, look up to me

and whisper, *you have changed,*

-- *and I love you more than ever.*

✦

my heart's arc — to be clear

In Love -- with him

In love with him

In love without him

In Love -- with or without

In Love

we say I love you

We say

into darkness,

i love you,

only to learn

there is no other.

We whisper

into shadows,

i love,

only to find

there is no i.

Until we sit

in Divine Light's

Silence,

realizing,

there is only Love.

✦

why speak at all?

There's so much noise in
unpremeditated words;
   yet in Silence is
where sweetness lies.

In a soft-eyes gaze,
a slight nod of the head,
gentle squeeze of the hand;
the e-lon-ga-ted blink.

When there are so
many ways to say
        I love you,
why speak at all?

I am whole

i am quick to remember pain,

for pain i know,

pain i know intimately.

But i must also remember joy,

for it is in joy

that i know intimately,

I am whole.

note from Self

Amidst this crazy world where
so many die in the doldrums of desire,
you finally found your frequency,
the delicately delicious essence that is –– You.

Now guard it fiercely, you living temple.

The world doesn't need some approved of
sweetly appealing flaccid version of you.
It needs You! You wild ball of conscious stardust.
Prioritize your sanctity.

THIS place now

I need to live

from THIS place now,

where I can feel You

as close as blood

running through my veins.

It's not a want,

not now,

now that the umbilical of

forgetting has been severed;

THIS has become my oxygen

as necessary as

morning rays to dawn birds

as moisture is to moss.

when I say I love

When I say

        I Love...

don't pull me down,

finish my sentence:

chocolate, puppy dogs

... you.

watendlath beck

Today I walk, not in the world of human,

of greed, of taking -- of spite,

but in the land of Fairy fells.

A world carpeted in moss;

landmarked -- not by name,

but by turns in becks and juts in boughs.

Today I take solace in a world,

that gives, then receives, then gives again.

Where footfalls murmur thank-yous,

where sunlight nourishes hunger;

and lips are quenched by land.

Today I sing where no ears can hear,

where only heartwood can record my song.

For from here it is clear the need to

damn society's shackles,

to walk away from the hell

we've been taught to sustain.

Today I cry to feel You close,

in a flash of blue beyond sight.

To feel Your hands almost touch mine;

to watch Your light in smoke and

rainbows dance over my body,

mapping my way home.

Today I stand and stare at Watendlath Beck,

and I cannot move from this spot,

for beauty has stolen my breath

and my heart has taken root through my feet.

Today I see that heaven is untouched by i.

✦

gently gently

Gently gently,

to think, this is enough

to write, this is enough.

For the meek will morph and fly;

graphene is mistaken for gossamer.

The Tenalach heart slides through

the portal between stone and bark into

Terra Nova, where the reverent thrive

walking barefoot, sweetly sweetly.

Here, the quiet spoken are heard –– and believed.

Here, the ones who move slowly

have space waiting for them when they arrive.

Here, life is offered, the way left hand passes to right with

no feeling of loss, never taken, Poornamadah.

Here, there's sweetness in Kinglet's flittering on

Forest's breathless canvas. Sonograms of Junco trills are

painted upon Sky, punctuated with Flicker's quavers against

Crow's syncopated call linking their beloved Trees.

A masterpiece.

Gently gently.

starlit rain

May we dance to
notes of turquoise and
sing in starlit rain.
Weave words that
sprout in darkness,
life's antidote
to unbearable pain.

✦

precious flame

Flame of my heart,
cupped in my hands
a soft yellow duckling

delicate as a fontanel;
precious as the last match
on a cold night.

I wonder what tinder you need.
Will the oils of my own hand, mixed with the
breath of poetry, and wax of song suffice?

Barreling down Moors
in this turbulent tin can,
as Wind howls and lorries

threaten to push us off for good,
we jump and jive; swerve,
then suddenly stop.

You whisper,
If you take your eye off me
I will not survive.

I know,
if I put you down beside me,
separate from my cradling,

we both will extinguish.

＋

Fred's meadow

The world melts away here,

in the meadow where

Blackcap sings his melodious song,

the soundtrack to my heart's opening.

I am home again at the beginning

of another cycle,

and you, my Beloved Fred,

-- standing path side, puppy watching --

welcome me to sit, to breathe,

to quietly cradle old friends in kindness,

for you know all too well,

that time flattens mountains of emotion,

and dries up caverns of tears,

leaving grooves and exposing layers

the future will call beautiful.

Sun shines here

-- where my heart remembered --

where acorns sprout and

flowers give way to budding leaves;

where I write notes in foreign tongues.

And Fred, you stand patiently

as One with two arms,

always open for a hug,

your heart the place

where I whisper my prayers

and sing to you my secrets.

✦

Distilled light

Light distills Silence into language
the way dew drops form on tips of golden grass,
–– out of thin air.

Quenching a thirst on the tongue
of those who have lost taste for the mundane,
for those who perceive life as dancing stardust.

✦

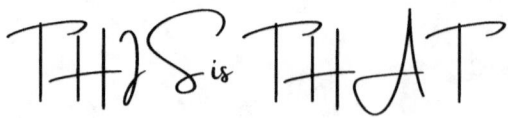

THIS is THAT

But what is THIS?

That is the question isn't it?

Both poison and pure water, it's

Amrit, an oasis and a mirage.

It's the yearning to hold a snowflake

in your hand made of stardust.

It keeps you striving forward

blindfolded in a room full of knives.

THIS gives hope and kills dreams

as it shakes you from the Maya.

It's Venus's heart firmly held in Saturn's hand,

a requirement; tethered to Butterfly wings

that fluttered in love lifetimes ago.

It's the sweetness in the inhale

after it's taken your breath away.

It's the shot of clarity just before you
jump off the cliff of duality.

It's just beyond the frustration of wonder,
into living without the need for reprieve.

It's thinking how much you love THIS moment
fully aware the moment's died
even before your thought is finished.

It is the Presence that pervades the spark of your person,
the fire of your soul, the light of a thousand Suns.

It's the power of a whole Universe
cradled in the nucleus of your being;
feeling it might blow at any moment,
knowing, it's your own Essence –– timeless;

THIS, it's the only thing worth living for.

THIS is written in the stars

Unable to side step

the portal needed navigating

upon a razor's edge of

before; of after, with

warp speed within.

To bring to Earth a present

that in Truth, was always here;

yet in reality, was forgotten

wrapped in the cloth of

'safe keeping',

to fester, to deplete,

to be rendered fallible.

But you, me, the Oneness that goes beyond;

the Eternal that makes us all, is here

to be remembered as Love

to be experienced as Life

to be embodied fully, for THIS

–– Love

THIS is written in the stars.